SHEIKH
MAKTOUM

LIFE AND TIMES

SHEIKH MAKTOUM

LIFE AND TIMES

BY ROYAL PHOTOGRAPHER
NOOR ALI RASHID

MOTIVATE
PUBLISHING

This book is respectfully dedicated to His Highness the late Sheikh Zayed bin Sultan Al Nahyan, President of the United Arab Emirates and Ruler of Abu Dhabi.

Other Motivate titles by Noor Ali Rashid

Abu Dhabi – Life & Times
Dubai – Life & Times
The UAE – Visions of Change
Sheikh Zayed – Life and Times

Published by Motivate Publishing

Dubai: PO Box 2331, Dubai, UAE
Tel: (+971) 4 282 4060, fax: (+971) 4 282 0428
e-mail: books@motivate.ae   www.booksarabia.com

Office 508, Building No 8, Dubai Media City, Dubai, UAE
Tel: (+971) 4 390 3550, fax: (+971) 4 390 4845

Abu Dhabi: PO Box 43072, Abu Dhabi, UAE
Tel: (+971) 2 627 1666, fax: (+971) 2 627 1566

London: Acre House, 11/15 William Road, London NW1 3ER
e-mail: motivateuk@motivate.ae

Directors: Obaid Humaid Al Tayer and Ian Fairservice

Text: Catherine Demangeot
Senior Editor: David Steele
Editor: Pippa Sanderson
Editorial Assistant: Zelda Pinto
Senior Designers: Johnson Machado and Andrea Willmore

Book Publishing Manager: Jeremy Brinton

First published in 2005 by Motivate Publishing.

© Noor Ali Rashid and Motivate Publishing.

ISBN: 1 86063 143 6

British Library Cataloguing-in-Publication Data.
A catalogue record for this book is available from the British Library.

Printed and bound in the UAE by Emirates Printing Press, Dubai.

All photographs by Noor Ali Rashid with the exception of the following pages: Al Bayan 8L, 44T, 45TR, 51T, 130, 131T&B; Department of Civil Aviation 99T&B; Wam 23, 45B, 47M(L&R), 47B(L&R).

T: top; B: bottom; L: left; R: right; M: middle.

Foreword

Maktoum bin Rashid: Prudent leadership and practical wisdom

In this important period in the history of the United Arab Emirates in general and the Emirate of Dubai in particular, His Highness Sheikh Maktoum bin Rashid Al Maktoum, Vice-President and Prime Minister of the UAE and Ruler of Dubai, stands out as an exceptional and distinguished political leader. His wise policies have led to the vast progress and prosperity in Dubai that place this city in its rightful place among the great cities of the world – a city with especially impressive accomplishments in the areas of commerce and finance. Under His Highness Sheikh Maktoum's leadership, Dubai has indeed become an oasis of development and progress. Continued growth and advancement have come to symbolise his blessed reign.

Sheikh Maktoum has had a most important role in strengthening the Federation of the United Arab Emirates and establishing its successful course. From his exulted position by our side as Vice-President of the country, his membership in the Supreme Council of the Federation, and his chairmanship of the Federal Cabinet, he has always been a strong and determined advocate for everything that strengthens the Federation and allows our country to fulfil its role and aspirations at the national, Gulf, Arab, Islamic and international levels.

The government and people of the United Arab Emirates are very appreciative of the leadership provided by His Highness Sheikh Maktoum and of his central role in our progress. We value his wisdom and his careful approach to decision making. We admire his hard work in the service of our country and our nation. If history judges great men based on what they offer their

countries, their people, and humanity in general, Sheikh Maktoum will be judged well. He has a unique place in the history of our country. His achievements, his works and his leadership have been instrumental to the modern renaissance of the United Arab Emirates. He is a person who embodies the important values of patriotism and love of country as well as loyalty and devotion to the Arab and Muslim nation.

Our people have a right to be proud of His Highness Sheikh Maktoum. He has helped make our country a unique example of excellence and success among the nations of the world. Thanks to his wise leadership, Dubai and the United Arab Emirates have achieved high levels of progress and prosperity. His continued efforts to help shape the history of the United Arab Emirates alone are sufficient to assure his place as one of our most important national figures.

Zayed bin Sultan Al Nahyan
President of the United Arab Emirates

Preface

Our greatest fortune in the United Arab Emirates has been that the leaders of our country are people of wisdom and vision. They have been able to see beyond the horizon and chart a path for our country's future. The subject of this important pictorial work, His Highness Sheikh Maktoum bin Rashid Al Maktoum is, without question, an embodiment of all of the qualities we admire in our leaders. He is one of the chief architects of the cultural, social and economic success of Dubai and the United Arab Emirates.

Indeed, the vibrant economy and the cultural achievements of this premier city in the Gulf are due, in no small measure, to his leadership in innovative planning. His energy, his vision and his commitment to excellence have enabled all of us to appreciate the role that Dubai and the United Arab Emirates play on the world stage. His support of all aspects of art and culture reflects his profound commitment to preserving the heritage and cultural values of our country. His ideas and aspirations are grounded in solid values and his commitment to his people is unshakeable.

As Ruler of Dubai and Vice-President of the UAE, Sheikh Maktoum is dedicated to achieving a state of stability, well-being and prosperity in Dubai and the United Arab Emirates as a whole.

These are the same goals that were at the core of the vision of His Highness the late Sheikh Zayed bin Sultan Al Nahyan, goals that have been articulated and strengthened by his son, and my brother, the President of the United Arab Emirates, Sheikh Khalifa bin Zayed Al Nayhan. As a result of this remarkable vision, development in the UAE has been successful and, indeed, very impressive.

We owe a great debt of gratitude to our leaders for their wisdom, their enlightenment and their hard work on behalf of our country and our nation.

It is therefore with great pleasure that I introduce this fascinating book about His Highness Sheikh Maktoum. The book is an enjoyable and informative photographic work compiled by Noor Ali Rashid, who has spent most of his adult life chronicling the major events of the United Arab Emirates' recent history through his images and, for more than 40 years, he has been the country's 'Royal Photographer'.

In this book, he uses his artistic talents and his camera to show Sheikh Maktoum as a leader, a nation builder, a statesman, a son and a father. The book portrays all this and more. Every page has interesting photographs that further our admiration of Sheikh Maktoum and his achievements. *Sheikh Maktoum – Life and Times* is indeed an important addition to the literature on the development and history of the United Arab Emirates. Readers will enjoy this opportunity to view aspects of a life that has helped shape our country for the better.

Nahayan Mubarak Al-Nahayan
Minister of Higher Education and
Scientific Research
United Arab Emirates

Contents

Introduction

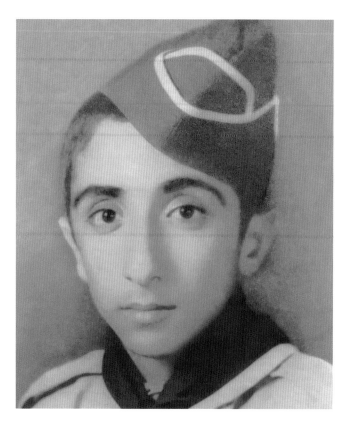

Sheikh Maktoum bin Rashid Al Maktoum is the ninth Ruler of a dynasty that stretches back more than 170 years. Its first Ruler governed a group of members of the Al Bu Falasah branch of the Bani Yas tribe that seceded from Abu Dhabi and migrated from the Liwa Oasis to Dubai, where they settled along the banks of the Creek. Soon after creating their settlement, the Al Maktoum family moved into Al Fahidi Fort, from which the *diwan* (Ruler's office) governed the affairs of the small community.

Trading with other parts of the Arabian Gulf coast and fishing featured largely in the life of the new settlement. But Dubai, as the settlement came to be known, would have retained a very modest size and influence had its successive rulers not seized every opportunity which presented itself – motivated it seems by the conviction that the emirate was destined for a grand future.

Sheikh Maktoum became the Ruler of Dubai on October 7, 1990, on the death of his father, Sheikh Rashid, 'The Father' of modern Dubai.

Sheikh Rashid's passing away may have marked the end of an era but never the end of a vision. Indeed, the emirate's ambitious development process has not been impeded or diverted from its course.

There are two main reasons for this: Sheikh Rashid had trained his sons from an early age to the skills and responsibilities inherent in their destiny; and, since becoming Ruler, Sheikh Maktoum has used his skills in inspiring members of the ruling family and the community at large to hold the course set by Sheikh Rashid. His sense of diplomacy is respected among the rulers of the other emirates, and he is known for his compassionate and fair handling of federal issues.

Sheikh Maktoum succeeded in taking the emirate to new heights, building on the leadership skills of his brothers to develop Dubai and enhance its reputation overseas.

Sheikh Maktoum has been groomed as a leader since an early age, making one of his first public appearances when he was 15. He became the UAE's first Prime Minister in 1972 (an office he transferred to his father, Sheikh Rashid, in 1979) and, following Sheikh Rashid's death in 1990, became the Vice-President and Prime Minister of the UAE, and the Ruler of Dubai.

Sheikh Rashid's rule could have been an impossible act to follow. Instead, the transition was seamless and, under his rule, Dubai has acquired a world-wide status unimaginable just a few years ago. In September 2003, for example, the world's eyes were turned towards the 'emirate in the desert' as it became the first Arab city to host the IMF/World Bank Annual meetings, lavishing its traditional hospitality on close to 15,000 visitors.

The apprenticeship of a Ruler

Even though Sheikh Maktoum was handed the reins of power relatively late in his life (at the age of 47), he'd been the Ruler-in-waiting for many years. He and his brothers had had to assume larger and larger responsibilities since the 1980s, when Sheikh Rashid progressively saw his health fail him.

Sheikh Maktoum was given responsibilities in the government in 1958 at the age of 15, upon the accession of Sheikh Rashid as Ruler. In fact, one of Sheikh Maktoum's first public appearances was on October 4, 1958, when he addressed the officials present at the ceremony marking the accession of Sheikh Rashid.

Photographs from the early 1960s show him at his office in the Land Department (see pages 56/57), attending meetings at the municipality (see pages 58/59) and dealing with the day-to-day problems of the community. This very hands-on training, which followed several years of education in the United Kingdom, taught Sheikh Maktoum to consult, decide and resolve – the very same skills he would put to use during the Federation meetings.

In January 1968, Britain announced that it would withdraw from the Gulf within three years. Britain had, since signing a series of treaties with the rulers of the different emirates in the 19th century, assured the protection of the

Since becoming the ninth Ruler of a dynasty whose reign is now approaching 200 years, Sheikh Maktoum has used his training and skills – together with those of his brothers – in taking Dubai to new heights and in enhancing it reputation overseas. Moreover, from 1990, Sheikh Maktoum has also performed his dual role of Prime Minister of the UAE with distinction.

region against the guarantee that no other foreign power would be given concessions in the territory. The area concerned by these treaties came to be known as 'The Trucial States' and included the countries now known as Bahrain, Oman, Qatar and the UAE.

Immediately after the withdrawal announcement, Sheikh Zayed and Sheikh Rashid decided to press ahead with the union process. They forged the way by resolving outstanding issues concerning the union between the two governments. In these discussions, Sheikh Maktoum became the key negotiator, often travelling to Abu Dhabi for meetings with Sheikh Zayed and the Abu Dhabi government. It took just six weeks for an agreement to be reached and, on February 18, an accord was signed between Sheikh Zayed, who had become the Ruler of Abu Dhabi just two years earlier, and Sheikh Rashid.

The following three years were a period of intense diplomatic activity which led to the signing by six of the emirates, in July 1971, of a provisional Federal Constitution. Sheikh Maktoum was intimately involved with every step of the negotiations, developing in the process strong ties with the ruling families of the other emirates (see pages 40–43) and of Bahrain and Qatar. The success of the political format of the UAE Federation can be traced back to its three-year gestation period. This time enabled the ruling families to get to know and respect each others' positions and for solutions to be reached to accommodate the different situations of each emirate within the general framework.

A half century of continuity and progress

Continuity also characterises Sheikh Maktoum's wider role in the Arab and Asian worlds. On his regular foreign trips, such as when he heads the country's delegation to GCC or Arab League meetings, he deals with leaders he and his father have known for many years.

Noor Ali Rashid's photographic records provide ample evidence of this strong continuity. For example, Sheikh Maktoum's ties with the royal families of Bahrain, Kuwait, Oman, Qatar and Saudi Arabia span five decades (see

While carrying out his varied official duties, Sheikh Maktoum has still managed to enjoy time with his family and the people of the United Arab Emirates.

pages 46/47). Yet, state visits and official meetings tell only one side of the story – the more informal get-togethers on the occasion of family weddings, or camel and horse races, have also enabled the leaders of the region to remain in close touch.

Two strong characteristics of Sheikh Maktoum's leadership style are loyalty and continuity.

Here again Noor Ali's collection shows the amazing continuity with which Dubai has benefited throughout the last half-century: photographs taken decades apart show meetings and gatherings of the same people or their descendents (see page 61).

This strong network of long-standing relationships has enabled Sheikh Maktoum to steer Dubai towards a future which even Sheikh Rashid would have probably found ambitious. In doing this, Sheikh Maktoum has relied on – and used to the full – the extraordinary talent, experience and vision of his brothers Sheikh Hamdan and Sheikh Mohammed, in particular, and leveraged the unwavering optimism of Dubai's business community, to give the emirate a robust international stature.

In a region troubled by momentous events, Dubai could have easily strayed from its course. Instead, by remaining steadfastly loyal to its Arab brothers and its Western allies, it has forged ahead, playing host to more business visitors, more holiday makers and organising more sports, cultural and business events than ever. If in the late 1980s only the well informed knew of Dubai, few are those now – the world over – who have not heard about the emirate in one connection or another.

Leaning on the city's entrepreneurial spirit

If one may be tempted today to think that Dubai's success story reads like a fairy tale, it's important to remember that it could have just as easily remained a peaceful and sleepy little village alongside the Creek. Dubai, in fact, had very few real 'breaks', but seized every one of them. As early as 1894 Sheikh

Sheikh Maktoum has carried out his many duties as Prime Minister of the United Arab Emirates and Ruler of Dubai with efficiency, dignity and compassion.

Maktoum bin Hasher, Dubai's fifth Ruler and Sheikh Rashid's great-grand-father, offered full tax exemption to foreign traders, thus welcoming to the southern shores of the Gulf a first wave of expatriates from Iran. In 1903, Sheikh Maktoum convinced a British steamship company to make Dubai the main port en route to or from India. As a result, by 1908, Dubai had become a thriving port, with 350 ships in Deira and 50 in Bur Dubai.

The 1930s however were a bleak decade for the area: the world depression affected the level of trade in the region, and the introduction of cultured pearls from Japan asphyxiated the pearl-diving and trading industry which, until then, had supported much of Dubai's economy.

Again, in the 1950s, Dubai's future came under threat when the Creek started to silt, threatening to close off the access dhows had enjoyed to the warehouses deep inside the natural harbour and therefore jeopardising the city's lifeline.

Sheikh Rashid saw no other option but to dig deep into the emirate's then shallow coffers to dredge the Creek and build a new airfield, to save Dubai's sea connections and expand its air links. He also ordered the construction of Al Maktoum Bridge, which opened to a then meagre traffic in May 1963 (see page 100).

These projects appeared at the time as three major gambles. Few people in the late 1950s or early 1960s would have seen in these the turning points in the development of Dubai.

But the banks of the Creek became lined with more and more dhows, warehouses multiplied, and more banks opened branches along the edge of the Creek. Trade grew and, in the ultimate break, in 1966, oil was discovered offshore. Noor Ali Rashid's archive documents the euphoria the discovery brought to the citizens.

He photographed some of them returning by dhow from an oil platform, where they had been able to see the 'miracle' for themselves. And he captured on film the large crowd that had gathered around Sheikh Rashid and Sheikh Maktoum near the Creek to witness oil flowing out of a pipe set up by the oil companies for the occasion (see page 83).

The history of Dubai's development from that point on is well-known.

Not only have oil revenues permitted the incredible increase in well-being of the population, but they've also spurred Dubai's development to the extent that it is today no longer reliant on oil.

Statesmanship, wisdom and compassion

For Sheikh Rashid and Sheikh Maktoum, the early 1960s had been about acting wisely, decisively and boldly to salvage and preserve Dubai's future. The middle period of the decade saw them preparing the blueprint for the transformation of Dubai – a mission made possible by the discovery of oil. But their attention had to quickly be directed towards the momentous task of forming a new country. When, on April 4, 1972, Sheikh Maktoum was sworn in as the country's first Prime Minister at the age of 29, he'd acquired experience few other world leaders could boast at such a young age.

Following Sheikh Rashid's death in November 1990, the Cabinet was changed again and Sheikh Maktoum became the Vice-President and Prime Minister of the UAE and Ruler of Dubai. His stature and experience as a statesman is certainly in evidence as many of Noor Ali's photographs show (see pages 22/23 and 34/35). Motivated as always by the need to reaffirm continuity and constancy, Sheikh Maktoum decided to appoint Sheikh Mohammed as his successor on January 4, 1995 – and to recognise Sheikh Hamdan's invaluable experience and contribution by appointing him Deputy Ruler. Respecting the past, leveraging the present and securing the future of the emirate form the essence of Sheikh Maktoum's governing style.

If Sheikh Maktoum's life is inextricably linked to the history of Dubai and of the UAE, Noor Ali Rashid's closeness to the Al Maktoum family also allows the reader a rare insight into the private life of a man with a genuine attachment to a simple and healthy life made of hard work, long-standing relationships with family members and a large circle of friends. Noor Ali's photographs show him in the residence he lived in as a bachelor (see page 118), at schools (see page 85), and enjoying riding (see pages 129) or watching horse or camel races. The photographs of his wedding to Sheikha Alia bint Khalifa Al Maktoum in 1971 (see pages 122–127) are evidence of how far his connections spread, with photographs showing guests from all walks of Dubai life, and dignitaries from other emirates and other countries in the region.

The wisdom of his rule and his national leadership can be linked to his profound connections with not only heads of state and royal families, but also the whole of the community. Noor Ali Rashid's photographs show him equally at ease with all, taking an equal interest in their lives and concerns. Wisdom and compassion have indeed pervaded every aspect of his life and rule.

The face of Dubai has been transformed during Sheikh Maktoum's lifetime and the city is now regarded as one of the most modern and dynamic in the world. It is also one of the fastest growing.

Historical landmarks

Sheikh Maktoum's political training started at the early age of 15, on the accession of his father, Sheikh Rashid, as Ruler of Dubai. He has since, in his roles as Crown Prince and then Ruler of Dubai and Prime Minister of the United Arab Emirates, been closely involved with every aspect of the political life of Dubai, the UAE and, further afield, the Gulf Co-operation Council and the Arab World.

ABOVE: Sheikh Maktoum bin Rashid Al Maktoum, aged 15, speaks at the ceremony marking the accession of his father, Sheikh Rashid (seated, right), as Ruler of Dubai, following the demise of Sheikh Saeed bin Maktoum Al Maktoum. Also present are Donald Hawley, the British Political Agent in Dubai, and Sir Bernard Burrows, the British Political Resident in Bahrain. This was Noor Ali Rashid's first photograph of Dubai's royal family. The speech was made in Customs House, immediately after the ceremony.

OPPOSITE PAGE: October 1958: On the occasion of the accession of Sheikh Rashid bin Saeed Al Maktoum as Ruler, the newly established Dubai Police form a guard of honour around his residence near the present-day *diwan*.

ABOVE: The days of the Union Jack are counted: Emirate and British leaders pose for a photo in 1965 after their annual meeting at the Political Agency in Dubai. Three years later, Britain announced its intention to withdraw from the region. Left to right: Assistant Political Agent (later Ambassador) Michael Tait, Sheikh Sultan bin Ahmed bin Rashid Al Mualla of Umm al-Qaiwain; Sheikh Saqr bin Sultan Al Qassimi, the former Ruler of Sharjah; Sheikh Rashid bin Humaid Al Nuaimi, the late Ruler of Ajman; Sheikh Ahmed bin Rashid Al Mualla, the late Ruler of Umm al-Qaiwain; an official of the Political Agency; Sheikh Shakhbut bin Sultan Al Nahyan, then Ruler of Abu Dhabi; Ali Bustani, the Arab Assistant to the Political Agency; James Craig, British Political Agent in Dubai; Sheikh Mohammed bin Khalifa Al Nahyan; Sheikh Rashid bin Saeed Al Maktoum, the Ruler of Dubai; Sheikh Humaid bin Rashid Al Nuaimi, the present Ruler of Ajman; Colonel Sir Hugh Boustead, British Political Agent in Abu Dhabi; and Sheikh Maktoum bin Rashid Al Maktoum.

OPPOSITE PAGE, TOP: Political Agent Donald Hawley, right, tries out the first telephone installed in the Political Agency in the presence of Sheikh Maktoum and an employee of IAL. The novelty of telephones has drawn a large crowd of interested onlookers.

OPPOSITE PAGE, BOTTOM: Left to right: Sheikh Rashid bin Saeed Al Maktoum; three of his sons – sheikhs Maktoum, Hamdan and Mohammed; Sheikh Mohammed bin Sultan Al Qassimi and Sheikh Khalid bin Mohammed Al Qassimi (Ruler of Sharjah) during a pre-Federation meeting in Dubai in the late 1960s.

ABOVE: Ceremonial grandeur on the occasion of the retirement of Colonel Carter (far right), Commander of the Trucial Oman Scouts. Dressed in ceremonial 'Number Ones' are (on the stage) Sir George Middleton, Political Resident in Bahrain and the new Commander of the Trucial Oman Scouts, Colonel Bartholomew. Also on the ground, second from right, Donald Hawley, Political Agent.

OPPOSITE PAGE, TOP: Sheikh Maktoum was an active participant in pre-Federation political life. Here he is seen deep in discussion with Political Agent James Craig while they wait for the arrival of British Political Resident, Sir William Luce, from Bahrain.

OPPOSITE PAGE, BOTTOM: Sheikh Maktoum and James Craig accompanied by (centre) Sheikh Saqr of Ra's al-Khaimah and (right) the Commandant of Dubai Police, Peter Lorrimer, welcome Sir William Luce at the foot of his aircraft. Behind them, the officer wearing sunglasses is Colonel Bartholomew.

ABOVE: This 1960s photograph of Sheikh Maktoum remained the official portrait of the Crown Prince for many years and was displayed in scores of offices throughout Dubai.

OPPOSITE PAGE: Sheikh Maktoum with Sheikh Rashid, who is about to depart for London to promote development initiatives for Dubai. Looking on is Sheikh Rashid's secretary, Ahmed Al Moosa.

OPPOSITE PAGE, TOP: A pre-Federation meeting of the Trucial States Development Council, chaired by the late Ruler of Sharjah, Sheikh Khalid bin Mohammed Al Qassimi (extreme left). Sitting next to Sheikh Khalid is Sheikh Rashid's legal adviser, Adi Bittar. Sheikh Saif bin Mohammed Al Nahyan is next to Sheikh Maktoum.

OPPOSITE PAGE, BOTTOM: Union House, Dubai, 1968: Sheikh Maktoum addresses the committee appointed to draft the constitution of the Federation. By July 1971, six emirates had agreed on a transitional constitution on the basis of which the United Arab Emirates would be governed from December of the same year. Ra's al-Khaimah joined the Federation three months after independence.

ABOVE: December 21, 2002, Doha, Qatar: More than 30 years after his first involvement in Federation matters, Sheikh Maktoum heads the United Arab Emirates delegation at the 23rd Gulf Co-operation Council (GCC) Summit. He is flanked, left, by his brother, General Sheikh Mohammed bin Rashid Al Maktoum, Crown Prince of Dubai and Minister of Defence of the UAE. Also seen – in the right of the photograph – is the UAE Minister of Information and Culture, Sheikh Abdullah bin Zayed Al Nahyan, in discussion with the UAE Minister of Foreign Affairs, Rashid Abdullah Al Nuaimi (in the second row).

ABOVE: Scenes from a meeting of nine delegations discussing the formation of the Federation of the United Arab Emirates, under the presidency of the late Sheikh Zayed, then Ruler of Abu Dhabi. The initial talks involved nine emirates: Abu Dhabi, Dubai, Sharjah, Ajman, Umm al-Qaiwain, Ra's al-Khaimah, Fujairah, Qatar and Bahrain. The representatives of Qatar and Bahrain later decided to form separate states. The talks generated great interest well beyond the region, as evidenced by the crowd of photographers and reporters who travelled from other countries to cover the historic occasion (bottom left).

OPPOSITE PAGE: The representatives of five emirates are seen here, as they leave a Federation meeting. They are, from left to right, Sheikh Rashid bin Ahmed Al Mualla, then Crown Prince and now Ruler of Umm al-Qaiwain; Sheikh Zayed bin Sultan Al Nahyan, Ruler of Abu Dhabi; Sheikh Saqr bin Mohammed Al Qassimi, Ruler of Ra's al-Khaimah; Sheikh Rashid bin Humaid Al Nuaimi, Ruler of Ajman; and Sheikh Rashid bin Saeed Al Maktoum, Ruler of Dubai.

ABOVE: Sheikh Maktoum was the UAE's first Prime Minister. He was sworn in in early 1972, in the presence of (bottom photograph) Sheikh Zayed, the first President. Sheikh Maktoum later transferred the charge of Prime Minister to his father, before taking over again in 1990, on the death of Sheikh Rashid.

OPPOSITE PAGE: In the presence of rulers and citizens, the national flag of the UAE is raised for the first time in the morning of December 2, 1971. The building in the background was the Ruler's Guest House in Jumeirah, and the venue of several Federation meetings. It is now known as Union House.

ABOVE: **April 2, 1972: Sheikh Zayed opens the first cabinet meeting, before leaving and letting Sheikh Maktoum take over the chair. Seated at the main table, clockwise from left to right are: Sheikh Abdul Aziz bin Rashid Al Nuaimi, Minister of Labour and Social Affairs; Dr Sheikh Sultan bin Mohammed Al Qassimi, Minister of Education; Sheikh Hamad bin Mohammed Al Sharqi, Minister of Agriculture and Fisheries; Sheikh Mohammed bin Sultan Al Qassimi, Minister of Public Works; Sheikh Mohammed bin Rashid Al Maktoum, Minister of Defence; Sheikh Hamdan bin Rashid Al Maktoum, Minister of Finance and Industry; Sheikh Maktoum bin Rashid Al Maktoum, Prime Minister; Sheikh Zayed bin Sultan Al Nahyan, President; Sheikh Mubarak bin Mohammed Al Nahyan, Minister of Interior; Sheikh Ahmed bin Khalif Al Suwaidi, Minister of Foreign Affairs; Sheikh Sultan bin Ahmed Al Mualla, Minister of Health; Sheikh Ahmed bin Hamed Al Hamed, Minister of Information; and Otaiba bin Abdullah Al Otaiba.**

OPPOSITE PAGE, TOP: **Sheikh Maktoum chairs the first cabinet meeting after the departure of Sheikh Zayed.**

OPPOSITE PAGE, BOTTOM: **A friendly show of affection between the new Minister of Interior, Sheikh Mubarak (left), and the new Prime Minister, Sheikh Maktoum, as they meet at an evening function hosted by Sheikh Zayed at his palace in Al Khawaneej, west of Dubai.**

Sheikh Rashid at the opening of the road tunnel under the Clock Tower Roundabout, the last time he was seen in public. Sheikh Rashid first became ill in 1981 but kept a strong hand in the affairs of the emirate until the end of the 1980s. When he died, there was a seamless transition of leadership because he had initiated his sons into the affairs of the emirate and the country since their early years.

Sheikh Rashid died on October 7, 1990. Just two days later, after receiving condolences at Za'abeel Palace, Sheikh Maktoum is seen planning national and government affairs with his brothers Sheikh Hamdan and Sheikh Mohammed. Sheikh Maktoum became the ninth Ruler of Dubai and, the following month, the UAE's Vice-President and Prime Minister.

Members of the Supreme Council preside over the opening session of the Federal National Council in 2003.
From left to right: The then Abu Dhabi Crown Prince and now President of the United Arab Emirates and
Ruler of Abu Dhabi, Sheikh Khalifa bin Zayed Al Nahyan; Ajman Ruler Sheikh Humaid, Ra's al-Khaimah
Ruler Sheikh Saqr, Dubai Ruler Sheikh Maktoum, Sharjah Ruler Dr Sheikh Sultan, Fujairah Ruler Sheikh
Hamad and Umm al-Qaiwain Crown Prince Sheikh Saud.

ABOVE: The members of the Federal National Council pose for a souvenir photograph on the occasion of the election of Saeed Mohammed Al Kindi as the Council's Speaker in 2003. Seated, from left, are: Sheikh Hamdan, Deputy Ruler of Dubai; Sheikh Khalifa, the then Crown Prince of Abu Dhabi and now the President of the UAE and Ruler of Abu Dhabi; Sheikh Humaid, Ruler of Ajman; Sheikh Saqr, Ruler of Ra's al-Khaimah; Sheikh Maktoum; Dr Sheikh Sultan, Ruler of Sharjah; Sheikh Hamad, Ruler of Fujairah; Sheikh Saud, Crown Prince of Umm al-Qaiwain and Sheikh Hamad bin Saif, Deputy Ruler of Fujairah.

LEFT: The opening session of the 13th Legislative Chapter, 2003, of the Federal National Council, Abu Dhabi. The 40-member house, which was established in 1975, examines and, if needed, amends all proposed federal laws. One of its main roles is to discuss the annual budget. Seen in the front row are, from left to right: Sheikh Ammar bin Humaid bin Rashid Al Nuaimi, Crown Prince of Ajman; Sheikh Hamdan bin Rashid Al Maktoum, Deputy Ruler of Dubai; Sheikh Sultan bin Zayed Al Nahyan, Deputy Prime Minister of the UAE; Sheikh Sultan bin Mohammed bin Sultan Al Qassimi, Crown Prince and Deputy Ruler of Sharjah; and Sheikh Hamad bin Saif Al Sharqi, Deputy Ruler of Fujairah.

Statesmanship

Sheikh Maktoum's close association with the affairs of the Emirates since pre-Federation days has made him one of the most respected and appreciated statesmen in the region. He has put his statesmanship to tremendous use in building a strong United Arab Emirates, and a strong Dubai. He has also forged close ties with the leaders of the UAE, the Arab World and, further afield, Europe, Asia, Africa and America.

Several decades separate the photographs on this spread but the gestures and the closeness of the relationship between the late United Arab Emirates President, Sheikh Zayed, and Sheikh Maktoum, always remained constant.

Above: Sheikh Zayed and Sheikh Maktoum relax during a break in Federation meetings in the late 1960s.

Opposite page, top: Affectionate greetings displayed between Sheikh Maktoum and the late Sheikh Zayed on the occasion of Eid.

Opposite page, bottom: Some of Dubai's citizens, including children, also have an opportunity to greet their rulers on the occasion of Eid.

This page: Strong, enduring personal ties bind Sheikh Maktoum to the rulers of the six other emirates, whom he has known since childhood. He is seen here with Sharjah Ruler Dr Sheikh Sultan (top left), Fujairah Ruler Sheikh Hamad (top right), Ra's al-Khaimah Ruler Sheikh Saqr (centre left), Ajman Ruler Sheikh Humaid (centre right) and Sheikh Zayed and Umm al-Qaiwain Ruler Sheikh Rashid (left).

Opposite page top and bottom: There is also, of course, a very special relationship between the royal families of Dubai and Abu Dhabi. In the top photo we see the present UAE President and Ruler of Abu Dhabi, Sheikh Khalifa (centre), and Sheikh Suroor bin Mohammed Al Nahyan (right) with Sheikh Maktoum at Sheikh Zayed's Qasr Al Bahr palace; in the bottom photo, Sheikh Maktoum converses with Sheikh Nahayan Mubarak Al-Nahayan at the same venue (Sheikh Khalifa is in the background).

41

ABOVE: Sheikh Maktoum with Ruler of Fujairah, Sheikh Mohammed bin Hamad Al Sharqi. The frequent gatherings required by the Federation meetings strengthened ties between the ruling families.

OPPOSITE PAGE, TOP: Left to right: Sheikh Hamdan, Sheikh Maktoum and Sheikh Zayed share a light moment.

OPPOSITE PAGE, BOTTOM: Sheikh Maktoum and Sheikh Mohammed meet with Sheikh Khalifa bin Zayed Al Nahyan, the then Crown Prince of Abu Dhabi.

Sheikh Maktoum has been involved in the emirate's foreign relations from an early age – an experience he brought to bear on his responsibilities at the federal level, and internationally in his dealings with other GCC and Arab officials. Sheikh Maktoum is seen here on a visit to Jordan (right), with King Abdullah of Jordan (below), with British Prime Minister Edward Heath and Political Agent Julian Bullard (opposite page, top left), with the late Egyptian President Gamal Abdul Nasser and Sheikh Rashid (opposite page, top right), and with Egyptian President Hosni Mubarak at Sharm al-Sheikh in February 2003 (opposite page, bottom).

THIS PAGE: Sheikh Rashid and Oman's Sultan Qaboos bin Said Al-Said at an official banquet (right). Years later, Sultan Qaboos welcomes Sheikh Maktoum at Muscat Airport (below).

OPPOSITE PAGE, TOP ROW: Sheikh Maktoum with the late Emir of Bahrain, Isa bin Salman Al Khalifa, and the current Prime Minister of Bahrain, Sheikh Khalifa bin Salman, during a Federation meeting in the late 1960s (left). The present King of Bahrain, Sheikh Hamad bin Isa, is Sheikh Maktoum's guest at the camel races at Nad Al Sheba (right).

OPPOSITE PAGE, MIDDLE ROW: Sheikh Maktoum on official visits to meet (left) Qatar Emir Sheikh Hamad bin Khalifa Al Thani and (right) Kuwait Emir Sheikh Jaber Al Ahmad Al Sabah.

OPPOSITE PAGE, BOTTOM ROW: Sheikh Maktoum with representatives of the Kingdom of Saudi Arabia: receiving Saudi Defence Minister, Prince Sultan bin Abdul Aziz Al Saud, at his Nad Al Sheba Palace in 1998 (left); and being received for a GCC meeting by the then Saudi Crown Prince (and now King) Abdullah bin Abdul Aziz Al Saud at Riyadh Airport (right).

TOP, LEFT: Sheikh Rashid (right) with the late King Hussein of Jordan.

TOP, RIGHT: Years later, in May 2000, Sheikh Rashid's son, Sheikh Maktoum, receives King Hussein's son, King Abdullah, at Nad Al Sheba Palace.

ABOVE, LEFT: Sheikh Maktoum with the Arab League Assistant Secretary Saeed Nofel (left) and businessman Hamad Al Futtaim.

ABOVE, RIGHT: At this widely attended 1969 event, Sheikh Maktoum sits next to Adnan Pachachi who, the year before, had been ousted by Saddam Hussein as Iraq's Foreign Minister and Ambassador to the UN. After 33 years in exile in the UAE, Pachachi returned to Iraq in 2003 and became a member of Iraq's Governing Council. Also attending the event are: (left to right) Sheikh Rashid; Kuwait's Representative in Dubai, Sheikh Badr Al Sabah; British Political Agent, Julian Bullard; and Ahmed Khalifa Al Suwaidi.

Sheikh Maktoum with: His Highness the Aga Khan, spiritual leader of the world's Shia Ismaili Muslims (top left); Indira Gandhi, the late Prime Minister of India (top right); Zulfiqar Ali Bhutto, then Prime Minister of Pakistan (bottom left); and General Zia Ul Huq, the late President of Pakistan – Sheikh Hamdan is also involved in the conversation (bottom right).

Formerly under British influence, Dubai still maintains strong links with Great Britain and, over the years, has enjoyed a number of visits from members of the British royal family. Sheikh Maktoum welcomes the Prince and the late Princess of Wales to Dubai during their visit to Kuwait, Abu Dhabi and Dubai in March 1989, and accompanies the Prince of Wales during an inspection of the UAE armed forces.

OPPOSITE PAGE: A portrait of a pensive young Sheikh Maktoum, taken at Dubai's Za'abeel Palace.

TOP, LEFT: Sheikh Maktoum escorts The Princess Royal, then Princess Anne; British Ambassador HB Walker and Sheikh Mana bin Khalifa bin Saeed Al Maktoum during the princess's visit to Dubai in the 1970s.

TOP, RIGHT: Albert, the Prince of Liège and Heir Presumptive to the Belgium throne (now His Majesty King Albert II), received by Sheikh Maktoum during his visit to Dubai in the 1980s.

ABOVE, LEFT: Sheikh Naif bin Abdul Aziz, Saudi Interior Minister holds talks with Sheikh Maktoum during his visit to the emirate in the mid-1970s.

ABOVE, RIGHT: Sheikh Maktoum with Sheikh Khalifa bin Hamad Al Thani (former Emir of Qatar), then Crown Prince of Qatar, during a series of pre-Federation meetings.

Sheikh Maktoum and other members of his family frequently visited Sheikh Zayed bin Sultan Al Nahyan
to discuss matters of national interest and enquire after his health and welfare.

TOP, LEFT: The late Sheikh Zayed clasps Sheikh Maktoum's hand on the occasion of Eid greetings. Seen as they leave the palace are, from left to right, Sheikh Saqr bin Mohammed Al Qassimi, Ruler of Ra's al-Khaimah; Sheikh Zayed; Sheikh Maktoum; Sheikh Humaid bin Rashid Al Nuaimi, Ruler of Ajman; Sheikh Hamad bin Mohammed Al Sharqi, Ruler of Fujairah; and Sheikh Hamdan bin Rashid Al Maktoum, Deputy Ruler of Dubai and UAE Minister of Finance and Industry.

TOP, RIGHT: From left to right: Sheikh Khalifa bin Zayed, Sheikh Saqr bin Mohammed, Dr Sheikh Sultan bin Mohammed Al Qassimi (Ruler of Sharjah), Sheikh Maktoum and Sheikh Saud bin Rashid Al Mualla (Crown Prince of Umm al-Qaiwain) during a banquet hosted by Sheikh Maktoum at his Nad Al Sheba palace on the occasion of the close of the camel-racing season.

ABOVE, LEFT: Sheikh Maktoum, accompanied by his brother Sheikh Hamdan, extends Eid greetings to the late President, Sheikh Zayed bin Sultan Al Nahyan at his Abu Dhabi palace.

ABOVE, RIGHT: Sheikh Zayed and his sons along with other family members warmly welcome Sheikh Maktoum at the Presidential palace.

OPPOSITE PAGE: Sheikh Maktoum with former Pakistani Prime Minister, Mohammed Khan Junejo, upon his arrival for an official visit to the United Arab Emirates in the mid-1980s.

Growing Dubai

Trade had provided Dubai with some degree of prosperity, but the discovery of oil in 1966 and its exploitation from 1969 enabled Sheikh Rashid to plan a whole new, grand future for the emirate. Sheikh Maktoum, from his first position in the Land Department's office, was involved with every step of the development of the emirate. In this life-long project, he has succeeded in harnessing the energy and commitment of his own brothers, Dubai's leading business families and, beyond, all of the emirate's citizens and residents.

ABOVE: Sheikh Maktoum at his desk in the Land Department, of which he was the Chairman in the early 1960s. The department was located in the former Souk Al Murshid area.

OPPOSITE PAGE: Sheikh Maktoum at work in his office in the Land Department in the early 1960s, discussing an issue raised by his visitor.

ABOVE: Dubai Municipality in the mid-1960s. Ahmed Al Ghurair is addressing the meeting. It involved both public servants and leading members of the community, who together were to shape the future of the city. The participants included, left to right: Dr Haris Mandodi, Abdul Ghaffar Hussain (foreground), Ahmed Al Ghurair, Sheikh Maktoum, Ghulam Abbas Ansari, Ali Al Sayegh and Saif Al Ghurair.

OPPOSITE PAGE: Accompanied by Ahmed Al Ghurair and Kamal Hamza, then Director of the Municipality, Sheikh Maktoum climbs the stairs of the old municipality building before the meeting.

Sheikh Rashid and Sheikh Maktoum have always closely involved merchants and businessmen in the affairs of the emirate, a strategy which has enabled them to quickly transform their plans into realities. Top row, left: Hamad Al Futtaim (second from right) in a meeting with Sheikh Maktoum. Top row, right: Sheikh Maktoum and Khalaf Al Habtoor. Middle row, left: With Juma Al Majid. Middle row right: With Obaid Humaid Al Tayer (and Sheikh Hamdan in the background). Bottom row left: With Mohammed Ebrahim Obeidullah (left) and Saeed Mohammed Al Ghandi (centre). Bottom row right: Sheikh Maktoum in conversation with Yousuf Habib Al Yousuf.

Close links between members of one generation have translated into strong relationships between members of the next generation. Top row: Sheikh Maktoum meets with Sheikh Shakhbut, the former Ruler of Abu Dhabi (left photo) and with Sheikh Khalifa, the current Ruler (right photo). Middle row: Sheikhs Maktoum and Mohammed with Sultan bin Sulayem (left photo), son of Ahmed Sulayem (right photo). Bottom row: Sheikh Rashid, Prince Philip and Ahmed Baker watch as Queen Elizabeth II unveils a plaque at the opening of Jebel Ali Port in 1979 (left photo) and Sheikh Maktoum greets Ahmed Baker's son, Tariq Baker (right photo). The director of Sheikh Mohammed's office, Musabeh Rashid, is in the background.

ABOVE: This aerial view of Deira in the 1960s shows an ambitious road infrastructure in place which, in turn, will facilitate other manifestations of urban development. Maktoum Street is connected to the airport road, using three major roundabouts to manage future traffic. Within a few years of this photograph having been taken, the landscape was dotted with multi-storey buildings.

OPPOSITE PAGE, TOP: Deira Souk, late 1960s. Dubai's focus on shipping and trade remains very strong, but concrete buildings and numerous cars indicate the first consequences of the discovery of oil.

OPPOSITE PAGE, BOTTOM: Just a few hundred metres further inland, on the Deira side of the Creek, near where the Twin Towers now stand, the scene is more serene – but Al Maktoum Bridge in the background is a sure sign of anticipated traffic.

ABOVE: This aerial view of Satwa and Jumeirah in the late 1960s shows lines of *barasti* huts, which were moved from the main Bur Dubai area to create a community that could begin cultivating vegetables for local consumption. In the distance, Port Rashid can be seen under construction.

OPPOSITE PAGE, TOP: Dubai Creek seen from Deira. Just right of the centre of the picture – facing onto the Creek – is the British Bank of the Middle East (now HSBC). Dubai's first multi-storey buildings, including that of Gray Mackenzie Shipping Company, can be seen in the background near the mosque.

OPPOSITE PAGE, BOTTOM: One of Dubai's first hotels, the Ambassador Hotel, can be seen at the top of this photograph taken in the late 1960s while, the waste land in front of it is now the location for the Central Bank building. On the left and hugging the banks of the Creek is the fish and vegetable market and, also shown, the Eastern Bank building in the centre of the picture.

Sheikh Maktoum visits Dubai's first jewellery exhibition, organised by Ahmed Siddiqi and Sons (Dubai's first major importer of jewellery and watches). The support and encouragement of trade has been an enduring constant among Dubai's rulers since the beginning of the 20th century.

As the economy developed so did the demand for goods and services. Early entrants into local production were the manufacturers of soft drinks. Here, Sheikh Maktoum, along with Sheikh Maktoum bin Juma Al Maktoum, is shown round a new Coca-Cola bottling plant.

TOP: The Carlton Hotel (the building on the right, facing the Creek) was the first hotel to be built in the 1960s and remained the most modern hotel in Dubai for many years. The 10-storey building on the left housed the Sahara Restaurant, Dubai's first night club.

ABOVE: The Citroen in this early landscape was the first French car in Dubai; it was given to Noor Ali Rashid by Sheikh Maktoum and therefore did not need a number plate. The tall building on the right is the Carlton Hotel, viewed from a different angle to that of the top photo.

OPPOSITE PAGE: Sheikh Maktoum with leading pearl merchant Ibrahim Al Fardan, who is wearing a string of pearls on his wrist. Before the advent of oil, pearling was the main industry in the Gulf.

ABOVE: A late-1960s nocturnal image of pearl trader Ali Al Owais' residence (centre). Note on the left a rather rudimentary resthouse – the forerunner to the Ambassador and Astoria hotels.

OPPOSITE PAGE, TOP: A late evening view of the Creek, taken from Shindagha in the same period. It is low tide, parts of the Creek haven't been dredged yet, and the water has receded away from the banks. At such times, it was possible to cross from one side of the Creek to the other on foot.

OPPOSITE PAGE, BOTTOM: An aerial view from approximately the same period shows the strong shipping activity which, until the Creek was fully dredged, remained dependent on the rhythms of the tide. The lonely building in the foreground, surrounded by sand, served as a public library.

A view of the Deira bank of the Creek taken from Customs House. Note the imposing windtower
houses belonging to the wealthier merchant families, surrounding a busy *abra* station. The reconditioned
ex-army Land Rover is waiting to be exported.

Dhows being offloaded in the 1950s in front of Customs House, located on the southern bank of the Creek, next to the Ruler's office. Some of the goods on the dhow in the foreground are stored in traditional pots. *Abras* transported some of the cargo to the souks.

TOP: This building housed the early vegetable (enclosed section) and fish (open section) markets in Bur Dubai. The fresh produce was brought to the market by *abra*.

ABOVE: This aerial photograph from the 1960s, which hung in many government offices, clearly shows the three distinct 'communities' which made up Dubai. Shindagha in the left foreground, Bur Dubai on the right, and Deira on the far side of the Creek. The city is growing apace and multi-storey buildings have started to appear in Deira. A newly surfaced road separates Shindagha from Bur Dubai at the same place where the communities were previously separated by water at high tide. Al Muraba watchtower, which still remains to this day, is visible on the left of the road near the Creek. The mouth of the Creek has changed considerably in shape since this photograph was taken – and continues to change – while the Deira Corniche has since been dominated by the tall Hyatt Hotel for a number of years.

Deira's Ras area in the mid-1960s, when Dubai was a town on the brink of change. Dhows still cluster along the shore and most buildings are just one or two storeys high. Nevertheless, a swathe of tarmac can be seen and the reshaping of the mouth of the Creek is well under way. The building in the right foreground housed a fish market while the other buildings near the water were the homes of wealthy merchants. Sheikh Maktoum, Sheikh Hamdan and other members of the Maktoum family attended Al Ahmediya School in this area.

ABOVE: The Creek in the 1960s. The dhow wharfage on the Deira side is lined with a new road. Within a few years, the open space on the right of the road would be covered with tall buildings.

OPPOSITE PAGE, TOP: When the dredging of the Creek was completed in the late 1960s, more and more dhows, mainly from the Gulf states, Iran and the Indian subcontinent, travelled to Dubai. The Creek and its warehouse area on the Dubai side soon became congested. Accordingly, in 1967, Sheikh Rashid ordered the construction of a deep-sea port. When it was completed it was called Port Rashid.

OPPOSITE PAGE, BOTTOM: With ample offloading space, large warehouses and the ability to handle large cargo vessels, Port Rashid – which was officially inaugurated in November 1970 – enabled the movement of goods to be conducted at a level that would never have been possible in the Creek.

ABOVE: Drafting new regulations for various government departments are from left to right: Kamal Hamza (then Director of Dubai Municipality), Sheikh Rashid, Adi Bittar (legal adviser to the Ruler's Office), Sheikh Mohammed and Sheikh Maktoum.

OPPOSITE PAGE: The first municipality office was situated on the upper floor of this building in the Bunder Taleb area of Deira. The ground floor conveniently faced on to a cargo-loading area for *abras*.

RIGHT: Sheikh Rashid (left), Sheikh Maktoum (second right) and Sheikh Hamdan (right) with Sultan Ali Al Owais (second left) and a Dubai education official at the opening of the first National Bank of Dubai building.

BELOW: Most banks in the 1960s were situated on the southern shores of the Creek. Seen here in the late 1960s are the long white building of the British Bank of the Middle East (left) and, next to it, the building of the Bank of Oman Ltd. Established in 1967, the bank changed its name to Mashreqbank in 1993.

OPPOSITE PAGE, TOP: The first branch office of the National Bank of Dubai, the first bank locally incorporated in the southern Gulf, in 1963, was situated next to the *abra* station and Captain's Stores. The bank staff had to ferry money across the Creek by *abra* each day.

OPPOSITE PAGE, BOTTOM: This photograph, taken a few years after the picture above, shows the arrival of the Eastern Bank (right) in a prefabricated building affixed to an existing building. The awning added to Captain's Stores provided some welcome shelter from the sun.

ABOVE: Oil was discovered offshore of Dubai in 1966 – a few years later than in Abu Dhabi – and production started in late 1969. This photograph was taken in 1966, when oil-company executives had arranged to have crude oil poured into a tank next to the Creek, as proof of the discovery of large reserves. Seen with the oil officials are Sheikh Maktoum, Sheikh Rashid (kneeling) and prominent citizens.

OPPOSITE PAGE, TOP: Sheikh Rashid and Sheikh Maktoum are shown a model of a *khazzan*: a tank in the form of an inverted funnel which stores oil in the sea. The oil, lighter than sea water, remains in the *khazzan* until it is pumped straight into a tanker. From the moment oil was discovered, Sheikh Rashid knew that he would be able to accelerate the pace of development. He immediately upgraded his infrastructure plans, including a new airport and a new port. But he also channelled the new-found wealth towards human development, in particular education and health.

OPPOSITE PAGE, BOTTOM: At the erection ceremony of the first onshore rig in Dubai. Sheikh Rashid is in the centre of the photo with Sheikh Maktoum, Sheikh Hamdan and Mehdi Al Tajir, former Ambassador to the UK, on his right; Mr Ripley, the first General Manager of Dubai Petroleum Company, is on his left.

OPPOSITE PAGE: The extensive grounds of the new Al Shaab School – the school which Sheikh Mohammed attended – stood at the junction between Shindagha and Bur Dubai. The discovery of oil provided for the education of a new generation of Dubai citizens who were later called upon to lead business empires. The area previously taken up by the school is now Dubai's main taxi stand.

LEFT: Sheikh Maktoum with Sheikh Mohammed and British Political Agent Julian Bullard at the Aisha Girls' School in Karama. Four of Noor Ali Rashid's children – Shams, Samia, Althaf and Naushad – are standing behind Sheikh Maktoum.

BELOW: Sheikh Maktoum with Zohdi Khatib (left), the teacher who supervised Dubai's first school, attended by children from the ruling and merchant families. To the right of Sheikh Maktoum is Khalifa bin Za'an, Chief of Security for Za'abeel Palace. Until oil provided the necessary financial input for schools, Dubai and the Northern Emirates had relied on Kuwait's generosity for the funding of education.

The municipality's investment in heavy equipment spearheaded the fast development of the city. With tarmac roads came higher speeds, accidents (above), and the need for the Police Department to invest in the first speed radars (opposite page, top left). The Fire Department also had to keep up with the development of the city (opposite page, bottom right).

Opposite page, top: Al Fahidi Fort in the early 1960s, surrounded by sand. The fort is now the home of Dubai Museum in a busy, built-up area of Bur Dubai.

Opposite page, bottom: This photograph, taken in the late 1960s, shows how the area has developed. The main Friday Mosque of Bur Dubai at the right is where Sheikh Rashid and his family used to pray and is situated on the same spot as the present Grand Mosque. The open ground in the front of the photograph developed in time into an area of showrooms housing textile wholesalers.

Below: This image, taken a few years later than the one on the opposite page (bottom), shows continuing development. The square between the fort and the mosque has become a car park, roads have been surfaced and cars are even being stored on the roof of a building. The girl's school situated in the top left-hand corner of the photograph has since been demolished, while the Fikhri Building has been renovated and is now one of Dubai's heritage buildings.

OPPOSITE PAGE, TOP: The early days of Dubai Airport: a small building surmounted by a short control tower, a ubiquitous Dakota and a few Land Rovers.

OPPOSITE PAGE, BOTTOM: Elaborate ceremonies marked VIP arrivals at Dubai Airport. Here a band marches past a Fokker Friendship aircraft.

ABOVE: Sheikh Maktoum on the apron of the airport, with a British Royal Air Force officer.

Left: Sheikh Rashid inspects a guard of honour with the late Hardan Takriti, then Vice-President of Iraq, on arrival at Dubai Airport.

Top: Watching the landing or take-off of an aircraft from the new upstairs terrace was a novel event for many of the citizens of Dubai.

Above: A number of hangars and extensions had been added to the airport's original building by the mid-1960s. In the background is the Al Bustan hotel, Dubai's only hotel with a swimming pool in the 1960s. The hotel used to host Christmas and New Year gala dinners and dance parties for expatriates.

OPPOSITE PAGE, TOP: The new terminal under construction at Dubai Airport. Behind the airport are Garhoud and Rashidiya, now sprawling office, factory, warehouse and residential areas.

OPPOSITE PAGE, BOTTOM: The new terminal, which was officially opened in 1971, provides evidence of the growth of air traffic between Dubai and distant destinations. The Bustan Hotel, long the leading Dubai hotel, is seen in the background, at approximately the same location as the modern Al Bustan Rotana hotel.

BELOW: King Hussein of Jordan, on his first official visit to Dubai, waits with Sheikh Rashid for the Dubai Police guard of honour to march past the saluting dias at the airport.

ABOVE: Sheikh Maktoum waits to welcome Sheikh Rashid on his return from a visit to Kuwait. Sheikh Rashid is followed by Sheikh Badr Al Sabah, Kuwait's official representative in Dubai, and Sheikh Hamdan.

OPPOSITE PAGE: Sheikh Maktoum accompanies Arab League Secretary General Mahmoud Riyadh to his aircraft on conclusion of his visit to the UAE. Behind Sheikh Maktoum is Mehdi Al Tajir.

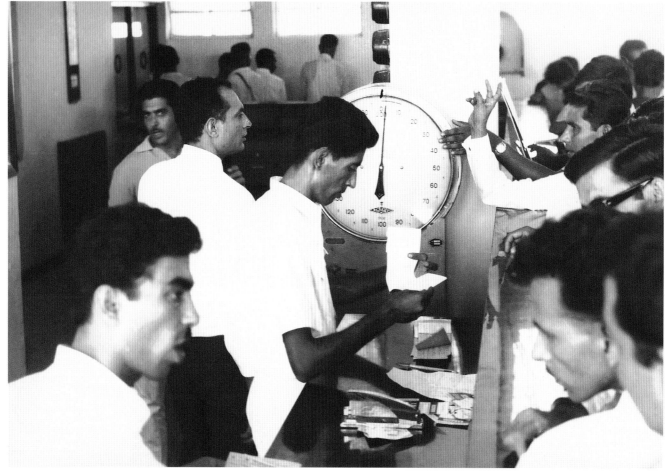

Opposite page, top: Staff awaiting visitors at an early immigration counter at Dubai Airport.

Opposite page, bottom: Pre-computer check-in procedures at the same airport.

Left and below: The Sheikh Rashid Terminal at Dubai International Airport, which offers passengers world-class facilities, was completed in 2000. A third terminal for the exclusive use of Emirates is under construction. More than 100 airlines take advantage of Dubai's open-skies policy, making it one of the world's busiest airlines.

ABOVE LEFT: This aerial photograph shows how much at the edge of town the Maktoum Bridge seemed to be in the 1960s. The Dubai side beyond the Creek-side palace of Sheikh Ahmed bin Ali Al Thani is very bare, apart from the first few rows of low-cost housing in Karama on the right and a few warehouses on the left; today, this area is the home of Rashid Hospital, Dubai Courts and a number of schools. Beyond, clusters of palm trees reveal the location of small settlements in Satwa and Jumeirah, and even the Jumeirah coastline is visible. It would only be a few years before these settlements formed one with the rest of Dubai. Shell oil tanks can be seen at right, on the near side of the Creek. They stood at approximately the same location as today's Dubai Chamber of Commerce and Industry and National Bank of Dubai buildings.

ABOVE: In this recent cityscape, taken from one of the high-rise towers on Maktoum Street, the Emirates Towers dominate a 'Manhattan' of other skyscrapers.

LEFT: As Royal Photographer, Noor Ali Rashid has enjoyed a long-standing relationship with Sheikh Maktoum, his father Sheikh Rashid, and members of the Al Maktoum ruling family.

TOP: With Sheikh Maktoum and his brothers, Sheikh Hamdan (front row, left) and Sheikh Mohammed (front row, right). Noor Ali Rashid's brother, Sultan Ali, is also present (back row, second from right) at this luncheon party hosted by Noor Ali Rashid in honour of Sheikh Maktoum and his brothers.

ABOVE: Noor Ali Rashid photographed with Sheikh Maktoum's sons, Sheikh Saeed (left) and the Sheikh Rashid (right), at Nad Al Sheba Palace in Dubai.

Family portraits

Having photographed the royal families of the Emirates for nearly 50 years, Noor Ali Rashid has had many opportunities to capture the specific moods and poses of Sheikh Maktoum and his closest relatives. Presented here is a series of portraits of Sheikh Rashid, Sheikh Maktoum and his brothers Sheikh Hamdan, Sheikh Mohammed and Sheikh Ahmed, as well as his son, Sheikh Saeed. Coming strongly across these portraits are rich feelings of optimism, confidence and humanity.

Sheikh Rashid – The Father of Modern Dubai – became Dubai's Regent in 1939 and officially took on the mantle of Ruler in 1958. He died in October 1990. He is widely credited with the visionary instincts which enabled Dubai to fully leverage every opportunity it was presented with and become one of the world's leading cities. He also introduced his sons to public life from their early years, thus ensuring the seamless continuation of his bold rule.

Sheikh Maktoum bin Rashid Al Maktoum became Crown Prince at the age of 15, on his father's accession in 1958, and Ruler in 1990. His father involved him from an early age in all affairs of the emirate, and he was an active participant in the political and diplomatic discussions which led to the formation of the UAE.

Sheikh Rashid placed Sheikh Hamdan, his second son born in 1945, in areas of responsibility from an early age. He was appointed as Chairman of Dubai Municipality and was trained in the areas of economics and finance. He became the United Arab Emirate's first Minister of Finance and Industry in 1972, a position he has occupied ever since, and Deputy Ruler of Dubai in 1995.

Sheikh Rashid's third son, Sheikh Mohammed, born in 1949, took a keen interest in the affairs of the emirate from an early age. He used his visits in the emirates and overseas to develop his vision for Dubai. He has been the UAE's Defence Minister since 1972 and was made Crown Prince of Dubai in 1995.

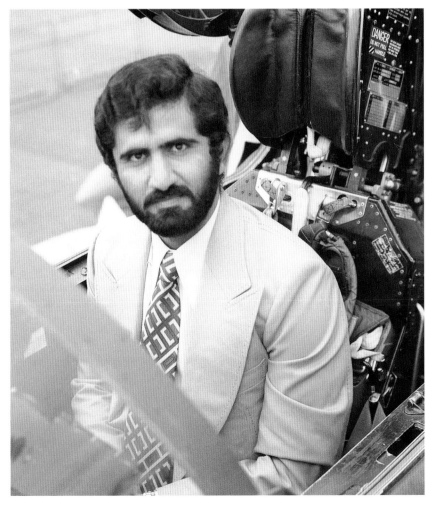

Sheikh Ahmed, the youngest of Sheikh Rashid's four sons, was born in 1950 and is a keen rider and horse owner. He has realised his passion for sport and action through a career in the military. A Major General, he is currently the Deputy Chairman of Dubai Police and Public Security.

Sheikh Saeed bin Maktoum, Sheikh Maktoum's eldest son, has grown to become, in his early 20s, a young man close to the community. He has a passion for falconry, shooting, hunting and football.

Milestones and passions

Sheikh Maktoum's personal life and passions have often blended with his public obligations. But his personal values and interests have pervaded every aspect of his life and work. The photographs of his wedding, a state affair, show his close ties to his people as well as to the dignitaries from the whole Arab world. In the course of satisfying his own passion for horses and riding, he now owns one of the most successful racing stables in the world, and has initiated one of the world's best-known horse races, the Dubai World Cup.

ABOVE AND OPPOSITE PAGE, BOTTOM: Sheikh Saeed's house in Shindagha, where Sheikh Maktoum was born. The house was built in 1896 as the residence and office of Sheikh Saeed, the grandfather of Sheikh Maktoum. Until the end of the 1950s, Shindagha had been Dubai's prime residential area. As Deira and Bur Dubai grew, the ruling and other families left Shindagha for more modern accommodation in Za'abeel, Nad Al Sheba and Jumeirah.

OPPOSITE PAGE, TOP: Sheikh Maktoum and Abdul Rahman Arif inspect a document handed over to them by Bill Duff, financial adviser to the Ruler.

117

LEFT: Sheikh Maktoum in his study in Za'abeel Palace in the early 1960s. Note the framed portrait of his grandfather, Sheikh Saeed bin Maktoum Al Maktoum, who ruled Dubai between 1912 and 1958.

BELOW: Sheikh Maktoum's desk in the working room.

OPPOSITE PAGE: A portrait of a relaxed Sheikh Maktoum, taken in the 1960s.

OPPOSITE PAGE, TOP: Sheikh Maktoum, Sheikh Hamdan and Sheikh Mohammed with Sheikh Ahmed bin Saeed Al Maktoum (partly obscured behind Sheikh Hamdan), Sheikh Marwan bin Maktoum bin Juma Al Maktoum (on Sheikh Mohammed's left) and Dr Khalifa Mohammed Ahmed Sulaiman (centre), await the arrival of the rulers at a banquet hosted in their honour by Sheikh Maktoum at Nad Al Sheba Palace.

OPPOSITE PAGE, BOTTOM: Sheikh Zayed and other rulers enjoy a banquet. From left to right: Sheikh Maktoum, Sheikh Hamad of Fujairah, Sheikh Saqr of Ra's al-Khaimah, Sheikh Zayed, Dr Sheikh Sultan of Sharjah, Sheikh Rashid of Umm al-Qaiwain, and Sheikh Humaid of Ajman.

BELOW: Za'abeel Palace in the 1960s and, across the road, Za'abeel Mosque. Za'abeel Palace was built by Sheikh Rashid and remains the favoured venue for royal-family gatherings and official celebrations. This area has seen large-scale development since this photo was taken.

ABOVE: Sheikh Mohammed and Sheikh Hamdan in discussion with Sheikh Maktoum during celebrations marking Sheikh Maktoum's wedding to Sheikha Alia bint Khalifa Al Maktoum in 1971. The photograph was taken at the traditional wedding breakfast held at his father-in-law's palace at Shindagha.

OPPOSITE PAGE, TOP: The bridegroom with Sheikh Zayed (left) and Sheikh Mohammed Khalifa Al Nahyan at Sheikh Zayed's Khawaneej Palace in Dubai.

OPPOSITE PAGE, BOTTOM: Sheikh Zayed and Sheikh Rashid with other officials watch the desert camel racing near Khawaneej on the occasion of Sheikh Maktoum's wedding.

ABOVE: Sheikh Maktoum's wedding celebrations were attended by many of Dubai's residents. One event saw Sheikh Hamdan (left) and Sheikh Mohammed (right), along with several other riders, switch horses in spectacular fashion while at full gallop.

OPPOSITE PAGE, TOP: Sheikh Maktoum and the Ruler of Qatar, Sheikh Ahmed bin Ali Al Thani, at the reception.

OPPOSITE PAGE, BOTTOM: Sheikh Zayed at his Khawaneej Palace with Noor Ali Rashid's eldest brother, Wazir Ali. Sheikh Zayed was in Dubai for Sheikh Maktoum's wedding.

ABOVE: Sheikh Zayed and Sheikh Mubarak lead a traditional dance during the wedding festivities.

OPPOSITE PAGE, TOP: Sheikh Ahmed bin Rashid Al Maktoum (right) and Sheikh Butti bin Maktoum bin Juma Al Maktoum were guests at the celebrations.

OPPOSITE PAGE, BOTTOM: The *mawleed*, a traditional chant, is performed at the wedding by guests close to Sheikh Maktoum, including (fourth from right) Abdullah Al Futtaim and (right) Humaid Al Tayer.

Below: Sheikh Maktoum has often turned to horseback riding in the desert for relaxation away from the affairs of state.

Opposite page: A keen rider and now also one of the world's leading racehorse owners, Sheikh Maktoum is seen holding the trophy for the US$ 6 million Dubai World Cup 2003 won by his horse, Moon Ballad. Also present are his brothers Sheikh Hamdan (also holding the trophy) and Sheikh Mohammed. In the bottom photograph he is seen congratulating a winner with Sheikh Mohammed.

ABOVE: At home and abroad, the Maktoum family's Godolphin racing stable has enjoyed great success, while the British Jockey Club has awarded Sheikh Maktoum its honorary membership for his role in raising the standard of horse-racing in Britain.

OPPOSITE PAGE: Sheikh Maktoum receiving trophies from Queen Elizabeth II (top) and Prince Charles (below).

OPPOSITE PAGE, TOP: Sheikh Maktoum and Sheikh Hamdan in discussion with camel traders.

OPPOSITE PAGE, BOTTOM: Some of these cameleers have traditional canes, others have rifles.

BELOW: The camel market behind Naif Fort, Deira, in the mid-1960s. A souk was later built in this area.

RIGHT: An enthusiastic group of children enjoy a live telecast of a camel race in the late 1980s.

BELOW: A decade later, tourists applaud at a camel race.

BOTTOM: A camel race in the 1960s.

OPPOSITE PAGE, TOP: Sheikh Maktoum with Sheikh Saqr bin Mohammed Al Qassimi, the Ruler of Ra's al-Khaimah, relaxing before a camel race in the 1980s.

OPPOSITE PAGE, BOTTOM: Camels were once the essential allies of the Bedu. They remain ubiquitous although many are now bred almost exclusively for racing and command very high prices.

The late President, Sheikh Zayed, enjoys Sheikh Maktoum's hospitality during the camel races in Dubai.

Sheikh Maktoum sits with his young nephew, Sheikh Rashid bin Hamdan, during the camel races at Nad Al Sheba, in the company of Sheikh Khalid bin Saqr Al Qassimi, former Crown Prince of Ra's al-Khaimah.

Family ties

Throughout his rule, Sheikh Maktoum has put to use the talents, energies and ambitions of many members of the Al Maktoum family. Concurrently, great emphasis is placed on the members of the next generation who, following a time-honoured Arabian tradition, are being groomed to assume future responsibilities.

ABOVE: Father and son: Sheikh Rashid and Sheikh Maktoum greeting guests at a banquet they are hosting at Za'abeel Palace.

RIGHT: Grandfather and grandson: Sheikh Rashid with Sheikh Saeed bin Maktoum at Sheikh Mohammed bin Rashid's wedding celebrations.

OPPOSITE PAGE: A young Sheikh Mohammed looks up to his older brother Sheikh Maktoum.

ABOVE: Forty years later, the brothers still enjoy a great deal of time together. Sheikh Mohammed's sons, Sheikh Maktoum (left), Sheikh Hamdan (second from left) and Sheikh Rashid (second from right) are also in this photo.

It is not just family ties, but also official responsibilities, which explains the closeness of Sheikhs Mohammed, Hamdan and Maktoum. The brothers are seen here during the UAE's first cabinet meeting in 1972.

In a more recent photograph than the one opposite, Sheikh Maktoum and Sheikh Hamdan receive Eid greetings from members of the United Arab Emirates community.

FOLLOWING SPREAD: Present and future generations: Sheikh Maktoum, Sheikh Hamdan and Sheikh Mohammed (centre group) with some of their sons. On the left are four of Sheikh Mohammed's sons, Sheikh Saeed, Sheikh Maktoum, Sheikh Hamdan and Sheikh Rashid; on the extreme right is Sheikh Maktoum's son, Sheikh Saeed.

143

RIGHT: Sheikh Maktoum's son, Sheikh Saeed, is seen with his uncle, Sheikh Mana bin Khalifa Al Maktoum.

BELOW: Sheikh Rashid (right) relaxes at Sheikh Mohammed bin Rashid's wedding celebrations with Sheikh Mohammed bin Khalifa Al Maktoum (left) and his son, Sheikh Saeed.

TOP LEFT: Sheikh Maktoum with his uncle, Sheikh Khalifa bin Saeed Al Maktoum.

TOP RIGHT: Sheikh Maktoum with Sheikh Mohammed bin Hasher Al Maktoum, Chairman of the Department of Justice.

ABOVE LEFT: Sheikh Mohammed with the late Sheikh Rashid bin Maktoum at Za'abeel Palace.

ABOVE RIGHT: One of the last photographs of Sheikh Rashid bin Maktoum.

Eid and other traditional religious and family occasions have enabled Noor Ali Rashid to obtain informal portraits of the members of the ruling family, often with their children. Above: Sheikh Mohammed and Sheikh Zayed, Sheikh Maktoum's two youngest sons. OPPOSITE PAGE, TOP: Sheikh Rashid with Sheikh Maktoum's daughters, Sheikha Metha and Sheikha Hassa, at Sheikh Mohammed's wedding celebrations. OPPOSITE PAGE, BOTTOM: Sheikh Maktoum with two of his nieces – Sheikh Hamdan's daughters, Sheikha Latifa and Sheikha Hassa. Sheikh Maktoum's son, Sheikh Mohammed, is in the background.

BELOW: During Eid, Sheikh Rashid visits his uncle, Sheikh Juma Al Maktoum (left) with his youngest brother, Sheikh Ahmed bin Saeed (right). Sheikh Ahmed is now President of the Department of Civil Aviation and Chairman of the Emirates airline group.

OPPOSITE PAGE, TOP: Sheikh Maktoum with his nephew, Sheikh Ahmed bin Mohammed Al Maktoum.

OPPOSITE PAGE, BOTTOM: Sheikh Saeed bin Maktoum (left) with his younger brother, Sheikh Mohammed bin Maktoum.

In March 2004 Sheikh Maktoum was bestowed with honorary membership of the Royal College of Surgeons in Ireland in appreciation of his contribution to humanitarian sciences in general and to health and medical research in particular. The ceremony was attended by his brothers Sheikh Hamdan and Sheikh Mohammed, as well as other sheikhs, ministers and dignitaries.